Teen Voices
Real Teens Discuss
Real Problems

Teens Talk About
Suicide, Death, and Grieving

Edited by Jennifer Landau

Featuring Q&As with Teen Health & Wellness's Dr. Jan

Rosen
YA™
New York

Published in 2018 by The Rosen Publishing Group, Inc.
29 East 21st Street, New York, NY 10010

First Edition

Library of Congress Cataloging-in-Publication Data

Names: Landau, Jennifer, 1961– editor.
Title: Teens talk about suicide, death, and grieving / edited by Jennifer Landau.
Description: New York, NY : Rosen Publishing Group, Inc., 2018 | Series: Teen voices : real teens discuss real problems | Audience: Grades 7–12. | Includes bibliographical references and index.
Identifiers: LCCN 2017019778| ISBN 9781508176541 (library bound) | ISBN 9781508176626 (pbk.) | ISBN 9781508176381 (6 pack)
Subjects: LCSH: Teenagers and death. | Suicide. | Grief. | Stress in adolescence.
Classification: LCC BF724.D43 T44 2018 | DDC 155.9/370835—dc23
LC record available at https://lccn.loc.gov/2017019778

Manufactured in China

The content in this title has been compiled from The Rosen Publishing Group's Teen Health & Wellness digital platform. Additional original content was provided by Adam Furgang.

Contents

Introduction

The loss of a family member or friend is never easy. Even under ideal circumstances, the teenage years are a challenging time of transition, physical change, and growth as teenagers develop from youths into adults. Teens must deal with a variety of social and physical changes related to puberty, social attachments, and new—often confusing—feelings. If a family member, friend, or mentor dies during this fragile time, the loss can have a profound and devastating effect on a teen.

However, losing someone close is not an uncommon experience for teenagers. According to data quoted by the Home Nursing Agency, one in five children will experience the death of someone close to them by age eighteen. In some cases, a child or teen may be touched by the death of someone whom he or she did not know well, such as an acquaintance or neighbor. This type of death may not require a lot of emotional adjustment. However, it can take a lot of time to recover from the death of someone close to us.

Dealing with the death of a loved one is one of the most difficult aspects of life. When someone commits

Losing a loved one can be devastating, but a friend or relative can offer support and guidance during this difficult time.

suicide, however, feelings of shock, confusion, sadness, anger, and even abandonment can be added to a person's grief. Many complex questions come up about how and why the person chose to end his or her life.

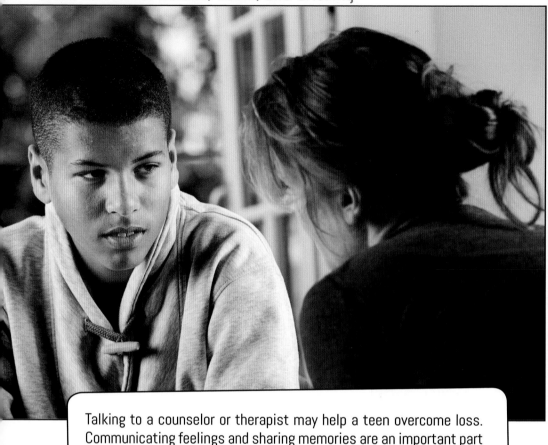

Talking to a counselor or therapist may help a teen overcome loss. Communicating feelings and sharing memories are an important part of the grieving process.

Some of the questions may never be fully answered by family or loved ones, making it even more difficult to accept the loss.

After the loss of a loved one, long periods of grieving and adjustment can take place. Normal daily routines can be upended by feelings of grief and sadness. Difficulty concentrating on chores or schoolwork, trouble sleeping, and even loss of appetite can all occur and are entirely normal. No one way of grieving is correct, but communication with friends, loved ones, and even professional therapists can all be beneficial so that

Share Your Own Story

The stories you are about to read were submitted by your peers to the Teen Health & Wellness Personal Story Project. Sharing stories is a powerful way to connect with other people. By sharing your story, you can connect with others who are dealing with these challenges. Find more information about how to submit your own story at the end of this resource.

the grieving person can learn to live with the loss and move forward.

The relationships we form with friends and family around us are an important part of our mental and physical health. According to a 2015 study in the *Proceedings of the National Academy of Sciences of the United States of America*, strong social ties help to reduce physical problems related to stress. These social ties help a person maintain a healthier weight, blood pressure, and stress hormone levels. The physical benefits of social contact may help a person through hard times, in addition to the emotional benefits these ties may offer.

Although it is impossible to prevent the loss of a loved one, there are healthy ways to deal with that loss so teens can continue onward in life. This resource helps teens take those tentative steps toward the future while acknowledging the pain that comes from the death of someone they loved.

Chapter 1

Teens Talk About the Death of a Parent

The traditional role of a parent in a teen's life is to provide stability and care. So when a parent becomes ill or dies, a teen's world can be turned upside down. Teens have various coping mechanisms to deal with the illness and death of a parent. Not all of them are positive, such as turning to drugs and alcohol. Some teens lose sleep, and as a result, their schoolwork and grades suffer. Some students are unable to focus on school because they need to start earning money for the family to help make ends meet.

Younger teens and older teens will grieve for a parent differently. Older teens may be able to talk about their feelings the way an adult would. Younger teens may have a harder time communicating their complex feelings and not know how to cope. They may require more guidance and need to see a therapist, either in a private session or as part of a group. Taking part in new activities with peers may help them get their minds refocused and away from their grief. No matter what positive steps teens take, grief is a process and

After the death of a parent, some teens are faced with new financial responsibilities. A teen may need to get a job to pay for college or household necessities.

they will need the time and space to deal with this overwhelming sense of loss.

Adelina's Story

Forever is a long time. It is impossible to measure and far-fetched to imagine. The idea that after death our souls will be eternal is difficult to comprehend. We live our lives with the constant reminder that eventually there will be an end, that our lives and the bodies we live in will finally cease to exist. The second part is believable as we have all lost someone or watched someone else lose someone. We understand that death comes to everyone. It's harder to imagine that life can continue after that stage because no one truly knows.

Memories are a funny thing. Sometimes we can never remember the things we want to remember and the things we try so hard to forget are the ones that stay with us for a lifetime. I have one of those memories. I was standing upstairs in my bedroom, nervously sharpening a pink pencil to a stub. That memory burns a hole in my mind because it was the moment before my entire life changed. It was the moment before the ambulance came with lights flashing and carried my mom away. Standing there, sharpening the pencil, I could see my life unraveling and I was terrified. More than that, I was alone. I knew then that forever was a long time to go without someone.

I spun the pencil around and around, watching it shrink until finally, there was nothing left.

I was young when my mom sat me down on the couch with my brother and sister and told us that she had been diagnosed with lung cancer. She told us that she was going to get treated and hopefully things wouldn't change too much. At first she was right. She started getting treatments and for a long time she was responding to them. She would continue to do the things that she would always do; and being a divorced

Finding out that a parent is seriously ill can be frightening, but keeping the lines of communication open may help the family deal with the diagnosis in a more effective way.

parent, that was a lot. But it was always there in the back of my mind: my mom was sick, very sick, and there was nothing I could do about it.

Some nights I would lie in bed and try to imagine "forever." It was a concept that I couldn't even begin to get my head around. Then I would try and think about life without my mom. I came up with the same predicament. I couldn't begin to imagine it. It seemed so impossible and unreal. Until it happened.

It was a few years later and my mom had been growing steadily worse. She had stopped responding to treatment, and she was growing very weak. My aunt had come to live at the house with us in order to take care of things since I was eleven and my sister was only nine.

This particular day, my sister was at a birthday party and I was at home. I was downstairs when I heard my mom cry out in pain, and I stood, frozen in place, as my aunt ran to grab the phone. As she dialed 911, I ran up the stairs to escape the chaos and frightening scene. Standing by my window, I could hear everything that was going on below me, the events that I was trying so hard to ignore. Dazed, I was praying it was only a nightmare; praying that I would awake in my bed and my mom would be lying in her room across the hall, healthy and well, praying that the last three years of my life had all been a cruel manifestation of my subconscious. Shaking, I grabbed a nearby pencil and started sharpening.

That was almost six years ago, and I still remember it like it was yesterday. I can remember the ambulance screeching to a stop in our driveway and the paramedics lifting my mom into the back of the vehicle. Reaching out, she grabbed hold of my hand and tried to smile at me through her pain. I can't remember if she spoke to me: I was too scared at that moment and everything seemed hazy. I didn't cry then, and I still didn't cry when I was at the hospital later to see her. I didn't cry when my dad showed up with my sister, and I asked him if she was going to be okay again. I didn't even cry when I left the hospital that night and went to my dad's house,

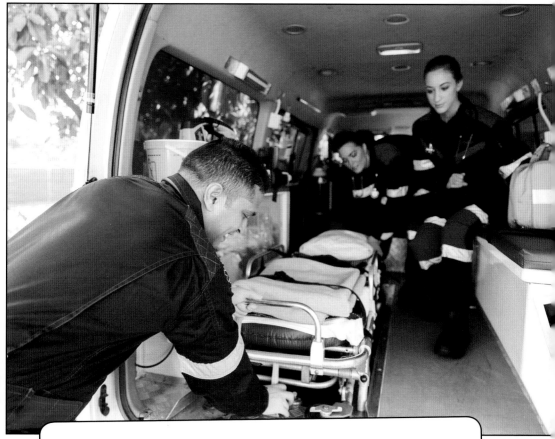

Watching an ambulance pull up to your home is scary, but paramedics are there to help those who are sick or injured.

leaving my mom unconscious in the hospital. I was too confused to cry. I didn't understand and nothing made sense. It didn't seem real, not until my dad told me that she had passed away. Then, I cried.

Not many people know my story. It isn't something that is easy to insert into a conversation. When I do have to tell people, it is a well-rehearsed version that I have become okay with telling; not my whole story. Not how helpless and scared I felt as I watched her leave me. Not how alone I felt without my sister by my side through it all. Not even a piece of how the sadness comes back to me at the most random times. But now I am telling my story. Now I am sitting here and reliving those feelings all over again. Pen in hand, I am writing out the things that have only been in my head for the last six years. Surprisingly, despite how hard it is, it helps.

Six years later, I still miss her all the time. I am painfully aware of how much I have to do without her, the things I have to learn on my own, and the memories I will have that she will not be part of. And I will still miss her for the rest of my life. That will never change, but I will also become a stronger person. At a young age, I learned the tragic lesson of loss. I learned how to cope, how to move on, and I learned how to remember.

The concept of forever is something that I do not think I will ever be able to understand. It is something that everyone has a different belief in and something no one can pinpoint for sure. The one thing I do know is that the belief I have developed for myself in the last six years has been the only thing that has kept me strong despite everything I have gone through. Looking back, I can still remember the foggy feeling I would get in my head when I tried to imagine life without my mom. Now, instead, I think of the concept of forever. Forever is a long time and the hundred years or less that I live in this body is only a tiny piece of it. After life there has to be something else, some way that our souls spend the rest of "forever," and I fully intend to spend it with my mom.

Looking at pictures of a friend or family member who has died can be painful but may also spark memories of happier times together.

Casey's Story

I never realized how precious life is until one day it really hit me. It can take a while to sink in, but it really hurts the most when you realize someone's gone. Losing my dad recently helped me realize this fact. He died when he was only fifty-one. That was young, but he wouldn't have wanted to stay in a hospital with lots of doctors helping him. We were hoping for a miracle, but one wouldn't come our way. Now we all realize how precious life is.

I always enjoyed waiting after school for my dad to come get me from school. It was the one thing I looked forward to every day. We had so much fun in our ten-minute ride, from talking to singing! Dad would sing in the funniest way possible just to see me smile. But one day as soon as I got out of class, I called Dad on my phone. No answer. I called him back a few minutes later, thinking he might just have been working on the farm. Still no answer. I called him quite a few more times, and when he didn't answer I called my mom. She said, "Try one more time and if he doesn't answer, call Grandma." I tried again. No answer from Dad. I called Mom back and told her I had no answer, so I called Grandma and she got me from school. When we got to my house, Dad's truck was in the driveway, so I thought maybe he was just taking a nap. But when I went in to look for Dad, he wasn't on the couch and he wasn't downstairs in the basement. I went back upstairs and saw him lying face up on the bathroom floor.

That is when I had the instinct to call Mom back and tell her. I told her, "Dad is lying on the floor surrounded by throw up and he won't respond to me." Mom said, "Hang up and call 911 now! I'm just getting off the interstate!" I did as I was told and called 911. I was in so much shock! That was when mom got home. The first responders and town police officer followed shortly after. About ten minutes later, the county ambulance got to our house. That is when they told us to get on the road to the hospital and they would meet us there.

Once we got to the hospital and were in the tiny waiting room, my mom, grandma, grandpa, and I were waiting for them to bring Dad into the emergency room. They still couldn't get Dad to respond on the way to the hospital. Mom and I got to see him for a few minutes, and then they told us he had to go back for a CAT scan. Just a little while later, they got the scans back on the computer and that is when the doctor came back with the news. She told us that he had a brain bleed and there was a lot of swelling. Mom and I were in shock! Mom said it was almost as hard as losing my older brother. Not long after the news, my sister and the rest of my family got there, and we told them what had happened.

Shortly thereafter, we were moved up to the adult ICU. There was a special room we got to stay in. After we got moved up there, the social worker talked to my mom and sister. I just couldn't get myself to go into the room and talk to her. Then I had to go in because they asked me if I would be comfortable talking to the

A hospital waiting room can be a stressful place for many people as they wait to find out the health status of their loved one.

child life specialists at the hospital. I told them yes, and my sister and I went into the next room. Once we were there, they explained everything to me in much calmer terms so it made much more sense. They let us pick out a blanket to put on Dad while we were there. We also got a handprint in special clay, and I got Dad's and my handprint to take with me to my ball games now. All of that was just super comforting to my sister and me.

After one day, I still couldn't get myself to go back and see Dad. It was hard on me especially because I was the one that had found him at home. At around 11:30 on Friday night after about an hour of crying I went in and saw Dad. He didn't look any different. He looked like Dad with a tube on his face; that's all it was. I wrote Dad a nice letter and colored him a picture. It was of a kitty. It looked like my kitty at home that would lie on Dad's feet when he was asleep.

After about five to six days in the ICU, they moved us to a different part of the hospital because we had admitted Dad into hospice care. About an hour after we left the ICU, a couple of friends came to visit me. I finally got to leave the hospital and see the outside world a little. After I went home, I went straight to bed. I was so thankful to sleep in my own bed. My mom called around 4:30 in the morning on February 15, 2012. She called to tell my sister and me that Dad had passed away.

We then had to start planning for the visitation and funeral. That was a very tough process on Mom, my sister, and me. But we got through it. We had visitation on February 19, and the funeral was on February 20. There were a lot of people at both the funeral and visitation. But we know that many people were Dad's friends, and many people knew and respected him. The funeral was the toughest part. We just wanted him back so much, but nothing could change.

So his life was in the hands of time after the accident. He meant a lot to everyone, even those who hardly knew him. He was a part of everyone, especially my sister, mom, and me. He has a special place in my heart. He will never be forgotten even though he had a short life. Now think about this: do you really know how precious life is?

MYTHS AND FACTS

MYTH It's better not to mention death or grief with a friend who has just experienced a loss because it will remind him of painful memories.

FACT It's important to communicate honestly with friends about death and grieving. Helping friends to express their feelings and remember a loved one who has died can be beneficial.

MYTH If your parent dies when you're a teen, your memories of him will eventually fade.

FACT Teens are old enough to have formed many lasting memories of meaningful people in their lives. These memories can last a lifetime.

MYTH If my parent dies of cancer, it is likely that I will also die of cancer.

FACT Cancer is not always fatal, and it is not always inherited. In the United States alone, there are millions of cancer survivors, and many cancers are not hereditary, or passed down to children.

Chapter 2

Teens Talk About the Death of a Grandparent

Grandparents can be an important figure in the life of a teenager. According to the Pew Charitable Trusts, in 2015 2.9 million children lived with their grandparents. This statistic shows that many grandparents are taking on the critical role of caregiver. For children who live with a grandparent, losing that core relationship can be especially difficult. Losing a grandparent may also be a teenager's first experience with death, and she might not be prepared to deal with the loss, especially if the relationship was a close one.

When a grandparent passes away, the death affects the entire family. Parents as well as teens grieve over their shared loss. Sometimes parents may be so wrapped up in their own grief that they are not able to offer the help or understanding a grieving teen needs. Friends and other family members can step in and offer support and comfort.

There are several ways to cope with the death of a grandparent. Talking about the grandparent and family memories is one way to work through

Grandparents are often the most important and involved extended family members in a teen's life. The bonds between grandparents and grandchildren can be powerful.

the grief. Remembering the grandparent's life and accomplishments can also be helpful. It takes time for everyone, especially teens, to work through the changes that can occur in their own lives when they experience such a heartbreaking loss.

Jane's Story

I lost my grandmothers to the cancer of August. Grandma Therese was like Mother Teresa, in the best

Grandparents often share their interests, including a love of the arts, with family members. When a grandparent dies, the grandchildren can take comfort in memories of time spent together.

sense. Grandma Jane V. shares my name. Each time her arthritic hands managed to write me a letter, I would laugh at the envelope that read "To: Jane V., From: Jane V." Both were children of the Depression. They were artists and readers, appreciated beauty, and were generous to a fault. These women raised eleven kids between them and truly valued education, especially the education of their girls. I will never forget them. Below are two poems dedicated to the lives of my grandmothers. I hope I'll make them proud.

When the Billows Spoke (for Grandma Therese)

The white blanched robe was pure.
Like Saint Therese.
Like Emily whose virgin lips had never tasted
A boy or a cigarette or a bottle.

Only Communion watered-down grapes and smoke
From his steak barbecues and burning incense on
Palm Sunday.
I saw on her palm a short lifeline.

You pricked me.
I felt the needles in your arm
Like I felt the pinch of the palm.

Palms are not for burning
But for the eaves of reeds. Thatched houses.
Mistaken for dandelions and blown down in wishes
with gusto.

I breathed into the plastic tube and it exploded
As my swimmer lungs made it satisfied.
I wanted to cut open my chest and swap my lungs
for yours
Because rattles are only for babies

We cracked the swinging door.
A saloon even within these holy walls.

I was the cross-bearer. The crucifer.
The gold was heavy like you.

*The higher I tried to lift it the deeper my heart retreated
into its cave.
I dragged it with one hand because the other was wiping
my eyes.*

*I saw them all. The strawberry-spotted handkerchiefs
and wiry frames
Sprinkling cracked desert faces.
We paced past.*

*The pallbearers carried her in a sleek black box.
I thought they called it a wake because she would wake up.*

*I touched her.
The fingers were frozen bloated sausages, sailors
with dropsy.
They sawed her ring off.
The billows spoke and I thought she twitched once.*

*I touched her eyelid.
I wanted to rip it back and make her cry.
To hit her like newborn babies to make her breathe.*

Jane V. I (for Grandma Jane)

*Her tiny house was white with
White walls and
White stucco siding and
White plush carpets and
White rocks in the yard, the desert grass, and
Her tufts of hair were white and
Her skin like wrinkled linens.*

*She scrabbled for red and blue mancala pieces
And dropped them one by one into the wooden puddles.
I wished I could swap the clear ones
For her eyes glazed over with glaucoma and cataracts.*

*Her fingers were too stiff to tickle the ivories anymore.
Mine trickled down the mess of blacks and
whites instead.
And she cried sometimes.*

*She cooked enchiladas so spicy
That I needed tortillas and
Glasses of orange juice to appease my tongue.*

*When I was barely in the double digits I was tallest.
I wished I was strong enough to lift her up into the
lemon tree
So we could squeeze some lemonade and laugh when
our lips pursed.*

*When I saw her she wore a vibrant yellow sweater
And she put on some makeup for the first time in months
Because she thought she would scare me.*

*I said goodbye to the cactuses
And to the lemon tree.
And the desert, cracked like my sunburned lips,
Got some salty rain.*

Ryan's Story

It was on a hot and sunny Friday afternoon in the middle of September—football season was in full swing—and our game was in a few hours. We had the day off from school. My girlfriend came over to hang out with me before I had to leave to meet the football team at the field house.

My grandmother was in the hospital that night, and my dad had flown to San Antonio early that morning because she was on life support machines. My grandmother had been in the hospital frequently since I was born, and I did not worry too much about it because she was a very strong woman. She always got through whatever was going on.

So, my girlfriend got to my house and not five minutes later, my mom called saying she was on her way home from work. She ordered me to get my brother and meet in the den. I knew something was wrong by her tone of voice. After that, I told my girlfriend that it would be best if she left. She knew what was going on, so she understood. My brother and I were sitting in the den, waiting for my mom and wondering what could have happened. I think we both had an idea but did not want to believe it.

My mother pulled up into the driveway and walked in and sat by the fireplace. She told us when my dad got to the hospital, he said a few words to my grandmother. Then my uncle and dad went to the cafeteria to get some lunch. My dad heard over the loudspeaker "code

Losing a grandparent may be a teen's first experience with death. The experience can be a real blow to a grandchild who was used to seeing his or her grandparent on a regular basis.

blue" and a room number, but he did not think anything of it. When they finished eating and went back to the room, the doctor said my grandmother went into cardiac arrest and died a few minutes after they left. Saying those few words to my grandmother were like a closing for my dad.

After my mom told my brother and me this, we started crying, and I did not know how to stop. I couldn't

A coach, teacher, or other trusted adult can provide the mentoring a teen needs during the grieving period after a loved one dies.

believe something like this could have happened. She was a loving, strong, and Catholic woman.

A few hours later, it was time for me to get my equipment and meet the team at the field house. I waited for the coaches to show up. The first coach there was Coach Watson. Right away, he knew something wasn't right about me. I told him what happened to my grandmother and started crying. He hugged me and said, "Whatever you need, I am here for you. No matter what it is, any time of the day, you can call me." He told me he too had one of his family members die during his football season, and I should play this game for her, like she is watching me. Even twenty years from now, I will remember those words.

After my team and I prayed, I said a prayer to my grandmother wishing she was there with me right now. I saw my dad walking onto the field. I ran to him and hugged him and started to cry, saying I was sorry. He said, "It is fine, Ryan. I just came to make sure you are fine."

During the game, it was like a dream. Knowing that something like this happened so early in my life. Although we lost, I cried after the game knowing that I played that game for my grandmother. Playing like she came to watch me and she was in my heart that night.

My family and I left days later for the funeral. It was a day I will never forget. Although I tried to hide the tears and be strong, I couldn't do it. I sat during the funeral, and I cried and could not stop. When it came time to bury her, I could not believe that it was real. I could not let go of the fact that my grandmother was dead, and this was her funeral.

One thing I have only told a few people is that the night before her death, I had a dream that one of my grandmothers had died. But I could not see which one it was. I think that is why I was not as shocked as everyone was because everything started to fit together. The one thing I regret is that when I saw her a month before she died, I never thanked her for paying for my schooling and baseball lessons. And I wish I could have told her how grateful and thankful I am for her doing this and how it meant everything to me.

This whole season, everything I have done is for my grandmother and everything I have done in sports is for what my grandmother has done for me. I will never be thankful enough for what she did for me. And I wish she was still here so I could thank her at graduation. I will always have my grandmother in my heart, and I will always love her and miss her.

Ask Dr. Jan

Dear Dr. Jan,
When I was growing up, I cried a lot and because of that now I hardly cry. Recently one of my friends died in a car wreck. I don't want to cry but I feel like I have to. Is this healthy, or is there another way to show my emotions?
— Aiden

Dear Aiden,

There are many healthy ways to express our feelings. The important thing to remember is that not expressing our feelings and keeping them bottled up inside causes significant emotional and physical harm.

Unfortunately most men are taught that it is a sign of weakness to express our emotions. Crying is often something that our culture dissuades boys from doing. But expressing our feelings is a sign of emotional strength and maturity. Whether you are male or female, crying is a normal and healthy way to express your feelings. That's why we often feel better after a good cry.

As I said, there are lots of different healthy ways to express feelings. The traumatic event of your friend dying in a car accident must be very difficult, and it is important to allow yourself to grieve. In addition to crying, which is completely appropriate, here are some other ways that you can deal with your feelings of loss:

- Journaling: A great way to get your feelings out is by putting them down on paper. This could be something that you share with others you trust or, if you prefer, just keep to yourself. By putting your feelings down on paper, it will help release them.

- Talking with a trusted friend and/or family member is a way to verbalize your feelings. This is a major reason that counseling is effective for so many people. It allows them to express their feelings and, by doing so, better understand them.

- Join a support group: There are support groups specifically for teens dealing with grief and loss. Many of these services are free or low cost. A good place to start would be to contact your guidance counselor, clergy member at your place of worship, or a mental health professional.

Whichever way you choose to express your feelings, it will lessen your pain and help you feel better emotionally and physically.

Chapter 3

Teens Talk About the Death of a Friend or Mentor

Friends shape our lives and help us create memories that last a lifetime. Mentors are people whom we look up to and who teach us what we need to know to become responsible, thoughtful adults. But when a friend or mentor dies, we can be left with feelings of emptiness and despair. For teenagers, the loss can be especially difficult because they have to deal with the changes that adolescence brings while managing their feelings about losing someone important to them.

While close friends are likely to be most deeply affected by the death of a friend, an entire community may need to come together to grieve and cope with the consequences of losing a young person or mentor.

School officials may let the school community know about the death of a student or teacher, and schools will often hold their own memorials in addition to private family funerals. Students and teachers will share stories about the person who has passed away and deal with questions about the difficult topic of death.

When a classmate dies, it affects the entire school community. Schools hold counseling sessions to help students process the emotions surrounding this tragic event.

People respond differently to loss. Some people may not want to talk about the loss of a close friend or a mentor in a public forum, such as a group counseling session. Other students may find it beneficial to discuss their loss openly. With this in mind, school administrators often offer grief counseling to help students deal with the crisis of losing a teacher or fellow student.

Chad's Story

January 12, 2010, was a day I will never forget. That was the day I lost one of my close friends, Carson, to brain cancer. We had been close friends since the age of four. He and I met in preschool and developed a great friendship. Carson was always one of the smaller kids, but that didn't stop him from running faster, jumping higher, and throwing the football farther than anyone else. He was just an all-around incredible athlete from an early age. He excelled in sports all through his early childhood and through middle school.

After homecoming freshman year, Carson's life changed forever. He was diagnosed with a rare form of brain cancer. Carson was unique in that he wasn't going to let cancer define him. He wasn't going to be known as the kid with cancer, and he wouldn't let it run his life. He fought his entire battle with that outlook. Freshman and sophomore year, I played in a Wipe Out Kids' Cancer golf tournament with him and some close friends. I felt so privileged to play in the tournament for him.

Throughout these last three years, he was able to travel all over the world and meet all different types of sport figures and celebrities. But something that I will never forget is when people said how cool it would be to have those experiences, he just responded with, "I would give it all back to be without cancer." He fought cancer with all the tenacity in the world. There was no way he was going to let cancer control him. He even had a bumper sticker in his room that said, "stupid cancer." To me, that shows how positive he was, and how he

In this 2015 photo, thirteen-year-old Reece King writes a wish to Santa at a Macy's store in Louisville, Kentucky, as part of a campaign to raise money for the Make-a-Wish Foundation, which helps children battling life-threatening illnesses

always kept his head up, even when things weren't looking good.

The day that he passed away, I was on my way to my second period of school when my friend approached me and told me that Carson had passed away early that morning. I just stopped. I couldn't say anything. I didn't know what to say, and I was speechless. I immediately called my mom and told her that Carson had died, and I was coming home. I left school and gathered

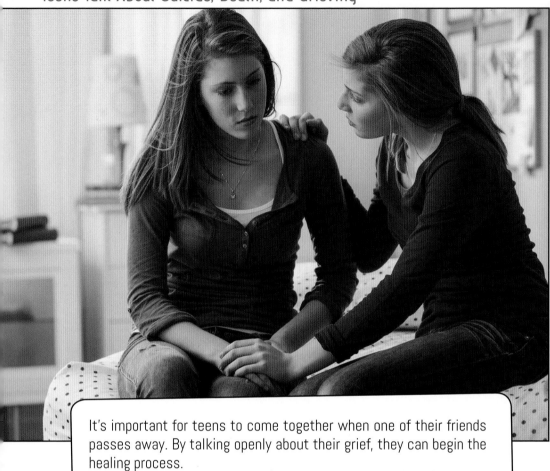

It's important for teens to come together when one of their friends passes away. By talking openly about their grief, they can begin the healing process.

at a friend's house, and for the next couple of hours we reminisced about all the good times we had with Carson. He taught me so much about dealing with adversity and coping with pain. He has changed my life for the better.

Madeline's Story

It was May 18, 2010, when I got that call. My memory is as clear as a bell: it was 4:45 in the afternoon. It was my coach who called, not about sports or work, but about loss and grief. It was then that I realized my dear friend had been in a car crash the morning before. We were both seventeen, and finishing our junior year, but only I would be able to see senior year. Only I would be able to experience college and a family of my own. A question I keep asking myself as I see my friends and my peers pass away is "Why them?" or "Why not me?" I saw my friend every day for two years, and now he is gone, like dust in the wind: there one moment and gone the next.

A couple of days later, I found myself at his school, Jesuit High, for his funeral. As I wrote my name down on the guestbook (along with my coach and other teammates), everything seemed so much more real than it had seemed before.

I took an aisle seat near the back and watched the sun glisten through the stained glass window of St. Peter. The service started, and the reverend and my friend's brothers talked about how he was a smart, joyful young man and how successful he was at this and that. All we could do was laugh. How could one not laugh at the stories of the adventures he took and the fantastic memories he gave us all? They talked about how he befriended everyone he met and made them feel special. Most of all, they talked about how he had joined crew with his school, and later on with my team. His brothers said how he impacted his friends through the team, but there was so much more to it than that. He taught me to never give up on what I wanted in life. If I really wanted something, I should always stand up and fight for it and never give up till I got it.

A memorial service or funeral service brings people together and gives them a chance to say good-bye to someone who has touched all of their lives.

That day, I did not just lose a friend, but I lost a great teammate and a great athlete. As the service ended, I sat in my seat for a couple minutes, looking at St. Peter. As it started drizzling outside for a moment, it looked as if St. Peter was crying, too. Right then and there, I knew everything would be all right, for God was showing his grief for our loss through a simple stained glass mural.

As my senior year nears the end, I finally figured out that my friend did not die for just any reason. But in a way, he died to show us how to live for what we believe in because we never know when our last day will be. In some way, he died for all his friends and me. Though we lost him, we grew stronger for having known him. We did not die because it is our job to realize that we should value what is given to us, as it can just as easily be ripped from our hands. We never know when we might be at our next funeral, saying good-bye to friends, family members, or neighbors.

Nine months to the day from my friend's death, as I write my name in another guest book, I am again reminded of how things never last. When someone leaves us and departs from this world, we open space for new life, for new stories, a new beginning. It is just a matter of how we live our lives.

Huck's Story

The sudden death of one of my school's most beloved teachers two days prior to opening day rocked our community. His absence made apparent how much he had affected his students and colleagues. A sophomore class advisor, soccer coach, faithful sports fan, and English teacher, he was a molder of young men and women and had a profound effect on all he touched.

The mood of the room changed when Mr. B arrived. Things immediately became lighter. He orchestrated sarcastic banter in the classroom and bellowed taunts from the basketball stands. He was not a man who sat back quietly. Apart from his charismatic personality, he was also a respected intellectual in the school's community.

Teachers can have a huge impact on a teen's life. When a beloved teacher dies, the sadness may feel overwhelming. Be sure to talk with a trusted adult about what you're going through.

I suppose that I knew him better than most people did, but when I heard of his death I felt surprisingly little sadness. The sorrow that I felt was for his family, especially his wife, my school's alumni director, whom he had recently married, and our head of school and his wife, who had become his in-laws just eight weeks before.

School started with a clash of emotions. Students and teachers rejoiced in their reunions after a long summer and held each other in sadness for their lost

Whom to Call

The following hotlines and organizations offer support to teens who are grieving the loss of a loved one or concerned that a friend or family member might be contemplating suicide.

Crisis Call Center
800-273-8255 or text ANSWER to 839863
http://crisiscallcenter.org/crisis-services
Twenty-four hours a day, seven days a week

National Institute of Mental Health Information Center
866-615-6564
http://www.nimh.nih.gov/site-info-contact-nimh.shtml
8 a.m. to 8 p.m. EST, Monday to Friday

National Hopeline Network
800-442-HOPE
http://www.hopeline.com
Twenty-four hours a day, seven days a week

National Suicide Prevention Hotline
800-273-TALK
https://suicidepreventionlifeline.org
Twenty-four hours a day, seven days a week

friend and colleague. The atmosphere was charged with emotion, both good and bad.

At the memorial service and reception later that week, all members of the school community were invited to mourn Mr. B's passing. I attended the reception along with my friends and family.

At the reception I looked around, examining other people's faces to judge the different reactions. I saw both tears and laughter as the mourners recounted memories of Mr. B. My own face settled into a tight-jawed scowl that made people look away when I made eye contact. Still, no tears came to my eyes. While my basketball teammates were teary eyed and red nosed, I was a statue looking out on a sea of sorrow.

Is my stoicism okay? If someone closer to me dies, will I feel sad? My uncle has been on death's door on and off for the last year. I have already accepted that he is going to die. When he does, will I feel the same way? I just don't know.

Chapter 4

Teens Talk About Suicide

In the United States each year, thousands of teenagers take their own lives. According to the Centers for Disease Control and Prevention (CDC), suicide is the third-leading cause of death for people between the ages of ten and twenty-four. Even though suicide is one of the leading causes of death among teens, it is still a shocking and devastating way to lose a loved one.

Overall suicide rates are also on the rise. According to the CDC, between 1999 and 2014 suicide rates increased for both males and females and for all ages between ten and seventy-four. The percent increase in suicide rates was greatest for females between the ages of ten and fourteen and for males between the ages of forty-five and sixty-four.

A person whose friend or family member commits suicide will no doubt feel sadness because of this loss. However, feelings of anger, guilt, or frustration may also be present—and may linger for a long time. A person who has lost someone to suicide needs to embrace whatever emotions come to the surface. Talking with other friends and adults is an important part of the

When a loved one commits suicide, a teen can cycle through many emotions. It's vital to get help dealing with the loss rather than suffering in silence.

grieving process and can help a teen come to terms with the impact that a loved one's suicide has had on his life.

Holly's Story

June 17, 2007. My best friend, Josh, took his life.

It was around nine o'clock at night when I got a call from his girlfriend asking me if I had seen Josh. I said no and went on with my night, playing pool and enjoying my time with my friends. I never stopped to wonder if my friend was okay.

A couple of minutes later, I got a phone call from Josh. I couldn't understand what he was saying. He was in hysterics and seemed to be speaking in gibberish, when in reality he was crying. I tried calming him down, but everything I said he didn't understand. I didn't understand. He said he didn't want to be here any longer? I brushed the thought of Josh committing suicide off my shoulder and said that if he felt that way he would have to relax. At that moment, he hung up on me. I stared at the phone for minutes in shock that my best friend had just hung up on me.

I went to sit on the couch. I laid my phone down on the table in front of me, hoping that he might call back. Still staring, my phone went off. "Float on down the river, float on down the river," it sang. I answered with haste, not looking at the caller ID.

I didn't say anything, but I could hear a slight whimper in the phone. It was Josh's younger sister, Anna. She had called to tell me that I needed to come over and talk to her brother. In confusion, I didn't reply. We sat there on the phone for a moment in silence. "I'm scared for him. I can't lose him. He's all that matters to me," she said to me.

Her voice was so soft, so frightened. I felt the anxiety began to bubble in my stomach. My vision began to blur. I stood up warily and left my friend's house, praying that everything would be all right. I walked down the street, trying to keep my balance. Everything around me was spinning. I could not handle the feeling in my stomach anymore. I ran.

Running faster and faster, my lungs started to burn. Tears began to pour out of my eyes, and mascara ran down my face. As I grew closer to Josh's house, everything finally made sense to me. I finally understood what Josh was saying: "I don't wanna be here anymore."

By that time, I was running as fast as I could. Thoughts poured into my mind. I am losing my friend, why didn't I take the time to listen? Why? Was he being serious? Is this really it?

I reached the front door, and Josh's dad came out and sat me down on the front steps. He wrapped his arms around me. I leaned my head on his chest. He told me that Josh loved me and cared for me very much, and he didn't mean to hurt me in any way. I looked up into his eyes, and I could see the pain he was feeling. He handed me a crumpled, disheveled piece of paper.

He left me on the doorstep and went back inside the house. I watched him walk in and saw Anna run down the stairs and jump into her father's arms. Weeping.

I stood up to walk away but remembered the piece of paper in my hand. I began to read. Josh had written me a note telling me that he did love life and that he did have great friends, but he didn't feel that his place was here. The letter explained that he wanted me to live my life to the fullest and to never look back, but to take each day one step at a time. Not to think too far into the future, but to live in the moment. I slid down the white column. I held the paper close to my chest. As close as I could get Josh to my heart.

I felt numb, lost, confused. I had lost a great friend, one that I thought I would have forever. But Josh did

A suicide note can have a devastating effect on those who are left behind. Friends and family touched by suicide will benefit from professional counseling.

what he thought was better for him, and left us, on paper, his brilliant mind. I cared for him and loved him dearly.

June 17, 2007. A remarkable friend, loving brother, and wonderful son took his life in order to teach the world the greater good of life—to live each day to the fullest and to gain knowledge of everything around us. He was my borrowed angel.

10 Great Questions
Ask a Grief Counselor

1. Why did this death have to happen to my family?

2. Why have I not cried after my parent died?

3. How do I stop people from treating me differently now that my friend has died?

4. My close friend has been acting odd. What are some warning signs of suicide?

5. I was always fighting with my mom before she got sick. Should I feel guilty now that she has died?

6. Could I get sick like my grandparent did and die, too?

7. Is it normal to be angry with my friend for committing suicide?

8. How can I memorialize my father now that he is gone?

9. How can I help my younger sibling who is very confused and upset by our parent's death?

10. Is it normal to want to be alone much of the time after losing a loved one?

The Teen Health & Wellness Personal Story Project

Be part of the Teen Health & Wellness Personal Story Project and share your story about successfully dealing with or overcoming a challenge. If your story is accepted for online publication, it will be posted on the Teen Health & Wellness site and featured on its homepage. You will also receive a certificate of achievement from Rosen Publishing and a $25 gift certificate to Barnes & Noble or Chapters.

Sharing stories is a powerful way to connect with other people. By sharing your story, you can connect with others who are dealing with these challenges. Visit teenhealthandwellness.com/static/personalstoryproject to read other teens' stories and to submit your own.

Scan this QR code to go to the Personal Story Project homepage.

Glossary

abandonment The action or feeling of being left alone.

administrator A person responsible for running a business or organization, such as a school.

cancer A disease caused by uncontrolled division of abnormal cells in the body.

counseling Professional guidance and support for people dealing with various life challenges.

depression A condition characterized by feelings of sadness, inadequacy, or low spirits.

diagnose To identify a disease or condition based on a particular set of symptoms.

forum A physical or online meeting place for the exchange of ideas.

funeral A ceremony honoring a person who has died.

grief Deep sorrow, often caused by someone's death.

hormone A chemical substance in the body that influences growth, behavior, or mood.

intensive care unit (ICU) A specialized unit of a hospital where severely ill patients are treated.

mentor A trusted advisor or teacher.

predicament A challenging, confusing, or dangerous situation.

puberty A period during which teens become sexually mature and capable of reproduction.

subconscious Relating to thoughts that exist outside of a person's level of consciousness.

suicide The action of killing oneself.

transition The process or period of change from one condition to another.

For More Information

American Academy of Child & Adolescent Psychiatry (AACAP)
3615 Wisconsin Avenue NW
Washington, DC 20016-3007
(202) 966-7300
Website: https://www.aacap.org
Facebook: @American-Academy-of-Child-Adolescent-Psychiatry-145459865751
Twitter: @JAACAP
The AACAP encourages the healthy development of families with young children and teens through advocacy, research, and education.

American Foundation for Suicide Prevention (AFSP)
120 Wall Street
29th Floor
New York, NY 10005
(888) 333-2377
Website: https://www.afsp.org
Facebook: @AFSPnational
Twitter: @afspnational
Instagram: @afspnational
The AFSP funds scientific research about suicide and suicide prevention, as well as provides resources and aid to those affected by suicide.

Canadian Mental Health Association (CMHA)
500-250 Dundas Street
West Toronto, ON M5T 2Z5

(613) 745-7750
Website: http://www.cmha.ca
Facebook: @CMHANational
Twitter: @CMHA_NTL
CMHA is a national charity organization that works to improve mental health for Canadians through community-based support resources.

Center for Grief, Loss & Transition
1129 Grand Avenue
Saint Paul, MN 55105
(651) 641-0177
Website: http://www.griefloss.org
The Center for Grief, Loss & Transition is a community resource center dedicated to the therapy and education of people experiencing loss, grief, and periods of difficult life transition.

National Alliance for Grieving Children
900 SE Ocean Boulevard
Suite 130D
Stuart, FL 34994
(866) 432-1542
Website: https://childrengrieve.org
Facebook: @NAGCnews
Twitter: @NAGCnews
The National Alliance for Grieving Children is an organization that provides resources for children and teens suffering from the loss of a loved one.

National Alliance on Mental Illness (NAMI)
3803 N. Fairfax Drive, Suite 100
Arlington, VA 22203
(800) 950-6264
Website: https://www.nami.org
Facebook: @NAMI
Twitter: @NAMICommunicate
Instagram: @namicommunicate
The aim of NAMI is to advocate for people with mental
    illness and to provide emotional and practical support
    for those dealing with mental health issues, as well as
    for their families.

National Center for School Crisis and Bereavement
(NCSCB)
1150 South Olive Street
Suite 1400
Los Angeles, CA 90015
(877)-53-NCSCB (1-877-536-2722)
Website: https://www.schoolcrisiscenter.org
Facebook: @uscncscb
Twitter: @schoolcrisisorg
NCSCB provides aid for schools in supporting students
    who have suffered a loss from any cause, including
    suicide or mass shooting.

Teen Health & Wellness
29 East 21st Street
New York, NY 10010
(877) 381-6649

Website: http://www.teenhealthandwellness.com
App: Teen Hotlines
Teen Health & Wellness provides nonjudgmental, straightforward, curricular, and self-help support on topics such as diseases, drugs and alcohol, nutrition, mental health, suicide and bullying, green living, and LGBTQ+ issues. Its free Teen Hotlines app provides a concise list of hotlines, help lines, and information lines on the subjects that affect teens most.

Websites

Because of the changing nature of internet links, Rosen Publishing has developed an online list of websites related to the subject of this book. This site is updated regularly. Please use this link to access this list.

http://www.rosenlinks.com/TNV/Death

For Further Reading

Bow, James. *Straight Talk About … Dealing with Loss.* New York, NY: Crabtree Publishing, 2015.

Cartlidge, Cherese. *Teens and Suicide* (Teen Mental Health). San Diego, CA: ReferencePoint Press, 2017.

Goldsmith, Connie. *Understanding Suicide: A National Epidemic.* Minneapolis, MN: Twenty-First Century Books, 2017.

Hastings, Eric. *Teen Suicide: The Step-by-Step Guide to Coping & Dealing with Suicide.* Seattle, WA: Inphinity Books, 2014.

Hyatt, Erica Goldblatt. *Grieving for the Sibling You Lost: A Teen's Guide to Coping with Grief and Finding Meaning After Loss.* Oakland, CA: Instant Help, 2015.

Jordan, Jack. *After Suicide Loss: Coping with Your Grief.* 2nd Ed. Seattle, WA: Caring People Press: 2016.

Kidde, Rita, and Antoine Wilson. *Mourning a Death in the Family.* (Family Issues and You). New York, NY: Rosen Publishing, 2016.

Kornfeld, Jody, Kathy Furgang, and Sophie Waters. *Death and Bereavement.* (Teen Mental Health). New York, NY: Rosen Publishing, 2013.

Marcovitz, Hal. *Teens and Suicide.* (The Gallup Youth Survey: Issues and Trends). Philadelphia, PA: Mason Crest Publishers, 2014.

Peterson, Judy Monroe. *I'm Suicidal. Now What?* (Teen Life 411). New York, NY: Rosen Publishing, 2016.

Popowitz, Coral. *Grief Recovery for Teens: Letting Go of Painful Emotions with Body-Based Practices.* Oakland, CA: Instant Help, 2017.

Romero, Susan. *Teens Dealing with Death: Stories from My Students.* Seattle, WA: CreateSpace Independent Publishers, 2014.

Sedley, Ben. *Stuff That Sucks: A Teen's Guide to Accepting What You Can't Change and Committing to What You Can.* Oakland, CA: Instant Help, 2017.

Toner, Jacqueline B., and Claire A. B. Freeland,. *Depression: A Teen's Guide to Survive and Thrive.* Washington, DC: Magination Press, 2016.

Worth, Richard. *Helping a Friend Who Is Depressed.* (How Can I Help? Friends Helping Friends). New York, NY: Rosen Publishing, 2017.

Bibliography

"Adelina's Story." Teen Health and Wellness. June 2015. http://www.teenhealthandwellness.com /article/113/13/adelinas-story.

American Academy of Child & Adolescent Psychiatry. "Teen Suicide." Retrieved March 21, 2017. https:// www.aacap.org/AACAP/Families_and_Youth/Facts _for_Families/FFF-Guide/Teen-Suicide-010.aspx.

"Casey's Story." Teen Health and Wellness. November 2015. http://www.teenhealthandwellness.com /article/116/10/caseys-story.

Centers for Disease Control and Prevention. "Increase in Suicide in the United States, 1999–2014." Retrieved March 21, 2017.https://www.cdc.gov/nchs/products /databriefs/db241.htm.

Centers for Disease Control and Prevention. "Suicide Prevention." Retrieved March 26, 2017. https://www .cdc.gov/violenceprevention/suicide/youth_suicide .html.

"Chad's Story." Teen Health and Wellness. October 2016. http://www.teenhealthandwellness.com /article/115/9/chads-story.

Children's Grief Awareness Day. "Did You Know? Children and Grief Statistics." Retrieved March 12, 2017. https://www.childrensgriefawarenessday.org /cgad2/pdf/griefstatistics.pdf.

"Holly's Story." Teen Health and Wellness. October 2016. http://www.teenhealthandwellness.com /article/316/10/hollys-story.

Home Nursing Agency. "Children's Grief and Awareness Day." Retrieved March 16, 2017.http://www. homenursingagency.com/our-services/childrens -services/healing-patch /childrens-grief-awareness-day.

"Huck's Story." Teen Health and Wellness. June 2015. http://www.teenhealthandwellness.com /article/113/18/hucks-story.

"Jane's Story." Teen Health and Wellness. June 2015. http://www.teenhealthandwellness.com /article/113/14/janes-story.

"Madeline's Story." Teen Health and Wellness. October 2016. http://www.teenhealthandwellness.com /article/175/9/madelines-story.

National Alliance for Caregiving. "Young Caregivers in the U.S." Caregiving.org. Retrieved March 16, 2017. http://www.caregiving.org/pdf/research /youngcaregivers.pdf.

National Cancer Institute. "When Your Parent Has Cancer: A Guide for Teens." Retrieved March 16, 2017. https://www.cancer.gov/publications/patient -education/When-Your-Parent-Has-Cancer.pdf.

"Ryan's Story." Teen Health and Wellness. June 2015. http://www.teenhealthandwellness.com/ article/113/16/ryans-story.

Snelling, Sherri. "Caregiving's Lost Generation: The Nation's Children." Huffington Post, May 21, 2013. http://www.huffingtonpost.com/sherri-snelling /children-caregivers_b_3304815.html.

Tennessee Suicide Prevention Network. "Myths About Suicide." Retrieved March 16, 2017. http://tspn.org /myths-about-suicide.

United States Census Bureau. "Census Bureau Reports 64 Percent Increase in Number of Children Living with a Grandparent Over Last Two Decades." Retrieved March 26, 2017. https://www.census.gov/newsroom /releases/archives/children/cb11-117.html.

Yang, Claire Yang, Courtney Boen, Karen Gerken, Ting Li, Kristen Schorpp, and Kathleen Mullan Harris. "Social Relationships and Psychological Determinants of Longevity Across the Human Life Span." *Proceedings of the National Academy of Sciences of the United States of America.* Retrieved March 12, 2017. http://www.pnas.org /content/113/3/578.abstract.

Wiltz, Teresa. "Why More Grandparents Are Raising Children." The Pew Charitable Trusts. November 2, 2016. http://www.pewtrusts.org/en/research-and -analysis/blogs/stateline/2016/11/02 /why-more-grandparents-are-raising-children.

Index

A

abandonment, 5
acceptance, 6, 44
adjustment, 4, 6
adolescence, 4, 34
alcohol, 8
anger, 5, 50
anxiety, 47

B

brain bleed, 15–20

C

cancer, 10–14, 20, 36
cardiac arrest, 28
Centers for Disease Control
    and Prevention (CDC), 45
closure, 28
confusion, 4, 5, 13, 47, 48, 50
coping mechanisms, 8,
    21–22, 34, 38
crisis counseling, 35, 50

D

death, 4
 of an acquaintance, 4
 of a friend, 32, 34, 36–38,
    38–41, 46–49
 of a grandparent, 21–22,
    22–23, 27–31
 of a mentor, 34
 not crying at, 12, 13, 32
 of a parent, 8
 of a sibling, 17
 statistics on experiencing, 4
drug use, 8

E

expressing emotions,
    32–33, 35, 44, 45

F

forever, concept of, 9, 10,
    11, 14, 36, 48
friendship, 34, 36, 39
funerals, 19, 30, 39, 41

G

grandparents as caregiv-
    ers, 21
grief, 5, 6, 8, 20, 21, 32, 34,
    39, 46, 50
group counseling, 35

H

hospice, 19
hotlines, 43

About the Editor

Jennifer Landau is an author and editor who has written about psychological bullying, cybercitizenship, and drug and alcohol abuse, among other topics. She has an MA in English from New York University and an MST in general and special education from Fordham University. Landau has taught writing to young children, teens, and seniors.

About Dr. Jan

Dr. Jan Hittelman, a licensed psychologist with over thirty years of experience working with children and families, has authored monthly columns for the *Daily Camera,* Boulder Valley School District, and online for Rosen Publishing Group. He is the founder of the Boulder Counseling Cooperative and the director of Boulder Psychological Services.

Photo Credits

Cover wavebreakmedia/Shutterstock.com; p. 5 glenda/Shutterstock.com; p. 6 © iStockphoto.com/ClarkandCompany; p. 9 Eternity in an Instant/Taxi/Getty Images; p. 11 Letizia Le Fur/ONOKY/Getty Images; p. 13 michaeljung /Shutterstock.com; p. 15 Andreas Pollok/Stockbyte/Getty Images; p. 18 Tyler Olson/Shutterstock.com; p. 22 sirtravelalot/Shutterstock.com; p. 23 Ruslan Guzov/Shutterstock.comp; p. 28 Antonio Guillem/Shutterstock.com; p. 29 digital skillet/Shutterstock.com; p. 35 Monkey Business Images /Shutterstock.com; p. 37 Brian Bohannon/AP Images for Macy's; p. 38 KidStock/Blend Images/Getty Images; p. 40 BorupFoto/iStock/Thinkstock; p. 42 Huntstock/Thinkstock; p. 46 tommaso79/iStock/Thinkstock; p. 49 jarenwicklund/iStock/Thinkstock; interior pages graphic elements natt /Shutterstock.com.

Design and Layout: Nicole Russo-Duca; Photo Research: Ellina Litmanovich